D1163830

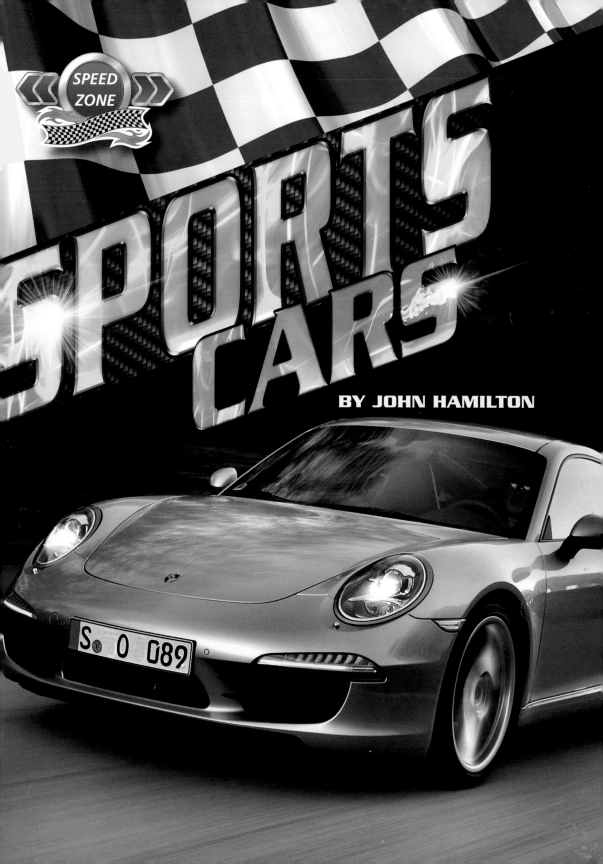

SPEED
ZONE

SPORTS
CARS

BY JOHN HAMILTON

Published by ABDO Publishing Company, PO Box 398166, Minneapolis, MN 55439. Copyright ©2013 by Abdo Consulting Group, Inc. International copyrights reserved in all countries. No part of this book may be reproduced in any form without written permission from the publisher. A&D Xtreme™ is a trademark and logo of ABDO Publishing Company.

Printed in the United States of America, North Mankato, Minnesota.
052012
092012

 PRINTED ON RECYCLED PAPER

Editor: Sue Hamilton
Graphic Design: Sue Hamilton
Cover Design: John Hamilton
Cover Photo: Corbis
Interior Photos: AP-pgs 17, 22, 28 (top) & 29 (bottom); Audi AG-pg 29 (middle); Automobili Lamborghini S.p.A.-pg 27 (top); Beverly Hills Porsche-pgs 18-19; BMW MINI Division-pg 29 (top); Corbis-pgs 10-11, 12-13, 13 (top), 16, 23, 26 & 28 (middle & bottom); DeLorean Motor Company-pg 9 (top); General Motors-pgs 4-5, 8, 20 & 21; Getty Images-pgs 6-7, 9 (bottom), 14 & 15; iStockphoto-pg 14 (logo); Jorge Ullfig-pgs 8 & 9 layout illustrations; Mazda Motor Corp-pg 27 (bottom); McLaren Automotive-pgs 24 & 32; Nissan North America-pg 25; Porsche Automobil Holding SE-pg 15 (logo); Thinkstock-pgs 1 (Speed Zone graphic), 2-3 & 30-31.

ABDO Booklinks
Web sites about racing vehicles are featured on our Book Links pages. These links are routinely monitored and updated to provide the most current information available. Web site: www.abdopublishing.com

Library of Congress Cataloging-in-Publication Data

Hamilton, John, 1959-
  Sports cars / John Hamilton.
     p. cm. -- (Speed zone)
  Audience: 8-15
  Includes index.
  ISBN 978-1-61783-530-8
  1. Sports cars--Juvenile literature. I. Title.

CONTENTS

SPORTS CARS

Some people drive cars just to get from place to place. Others drive for the fun of it. Sports cars were built for these driving enthusiasts.

XTREME FACT - Sports cars are built to look good. Their sleek bodies appeal to the public, and their aerodynamics help them achieve high speeds.

Sports cars are designed to look cool. They accelerate quickly. They have great handling, which means they can make tight turns even at high speed. They also have strong brakes, for quick stopping. Sports cars are simply thrilling to drive.

WHAT IS A SPORTS CAR?

What exactly is a sports car? Usually, sports cars are small and lightweight. They have powerful engines. This combination helps them accelerate quickly.

Sports cars sit low to the ground. They can take tight corners without spinning out. Most people say a true sports car should only have two doors and two seats. But there are some exceptions. Most of all, driving a sports car should be fun.

SPORTS CAR LAYOUTS

Layout refers to the location of a car's engine, driveshaft, and transmission. The placement of these heavy parts affects how a car handles during acceleration and high speed. Most sports cars have their engines near the front axle, with power driving the rear wheels.

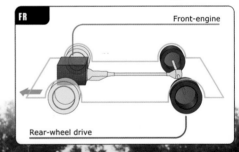

FR

Front-engine

Rear-wheel drive

Chevrolet Corvette

Some rear-wheel-drive sports cars have their engines in back. This gives the cars better acceleration and braking, but often makes them harder to handle.

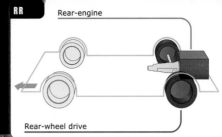

RR
Rear-engine
Rear-wheel drive

DeLorean DMC-12

Many extreme high-performance sports cars have their engines near the center of the vehicle. These mid-engine, rear-wheel drive cars have superb handling, but require much skill to drive.

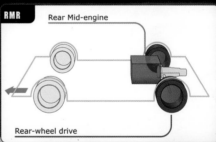

RMR
Rear Mid-engine
Rear-wheel drive

Lamborghini Miura

HISTORY

In the early 1900s, people wanted something more fun to drive than Model T Fords. Automakers from Germany, Italy, France, and Great Britain made small, fast cars. These "sporty" vehicles became very popular.

The Stutz Bearcat had a small "monocle" windshield.

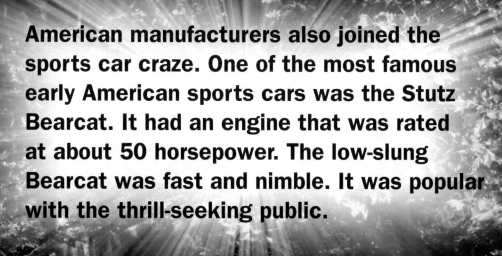

American manufacturers also joined the sports car craze. One of the most famous early American sports cars was the Stutz Bearcat. It had an engine that was rated at about 50 horsepower. The low-slung Bearcat was fast and nimble. It was popular with the thrill-seeking public.

XTREME FACT - In 1915, Erwin G. "Cannon Ball" Baker drove a Stutz Bearcat from San Diego, California, to New York City in 11 days, 7 hours, 15 minutes. His epic journey was called the "Cannonball Run."

After World War II, sports cars really began to catch on with the public. European automakers such as Jaguar, Porsche, and Ferrari created small, lightweight cars with streamlined designs. Today, sports cars are as popular as ever. Some people like to collect and restore classic sports cars. Others buy ultra-performing "supercars" that cost more than an average house!

The best-selling British Jaguar E-type Series 1 has often been named the number one sports car of the 1960s.

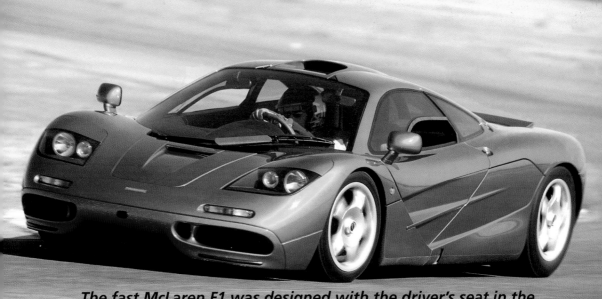

The fast McLaren F1 was designed with the driver's seat in the center of the vehicle, giving the motorist better visibility.

ENZO FERRARI

Enzo Ferrari (1898-1988) was a car designer and race car driver. In the 1920s he worked at the Italian car company Alfa Romeo. In 1947 he formed his own company. It has produced many famous sports cars, such as the Ferrari 250 GTO. The company's symbol is the famous Ferrari "Cavallino Rampante" ("prancing horse"), a black horse on a yellow shield.

FERDINAND PORSCHE

Ferdinand Porsche (1875-1951) designed the famous SSK sports car for German manufacturer Mercedes-Benz before starting his own company in 1931. He designed the Volkswagen Beetle, as well as the classic Porsche 356. Today, the Porsche company makes some of the most popular high-performance sports cars in the world.

SPORTS CAR RACING

Sports car racing is an exciting, popular sport. Cars are either specially built, or are heavily modified road vehicles. Races are held on tracks, called circuits. Most races last a long time. The winner is the team that endures hours of racing at very high speeds.

The 24 Hours of Le Mans endurance race takes place each year near Le Mans, France. It is the world's oldest endurance race.

Rally racing uses modified sports cars to race from point to point on specially laid out race courses. Drivers race against the clock. These grueling races are often held over several days in stages. Many are on rough roads, with course lengths of 1,000 miles (1,609 km) or more.

A Mini Cooper flies over a hill during a World Rally Championship in Portugal.

PORSCHE 911

The Porsche 911 series is often rated the best sports car of all time. This marvel of German engineering has been in continuous production since it was introduced in 1963. Its engine is situated in the rear. This gives the car incredible acceleration and faster braking.

Porsche 911
Turbo S

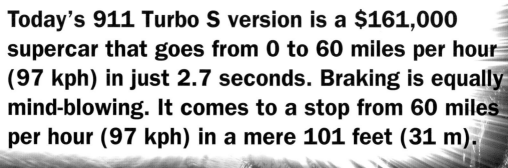

Today's 911 Turbo S version is a $161,000 supercar that goes from 0 to 60 miles per hour (97 kph) in just 2.7 seconds. Braking is equally mind-blowing. It comes to a stop from 60 miles per hour (97 kph) in a mere 101 feet (31 m).

XTREME FACT - The 1973 and 1974 Porsche 911 Carrera RS model is prized by sports car collectors. The RS stands for a German word that means "race sport."

CHEVROLET CORVETTE

The General Motors Chevrolet Corvette first appeared in the early 1950s and has been turning sports car lovers' heads ever since. It is by far the most famous American-made sports car. The stylish 1963 version, the Corvette Sting Ray, is still prized by collectors today.

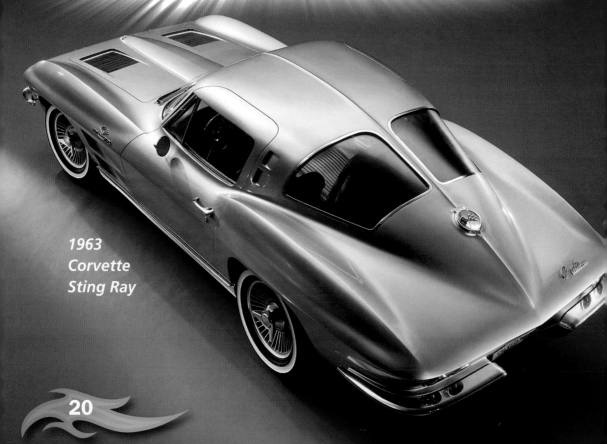

1963 Corvette Sting Ray

The 2012 ZR1 version has a breathtaking 638-horsepower supercharged V8 engine. It is one of the fastest high-performance sports cars in the world, with a top speed of 205 miles per hour (330 kph).

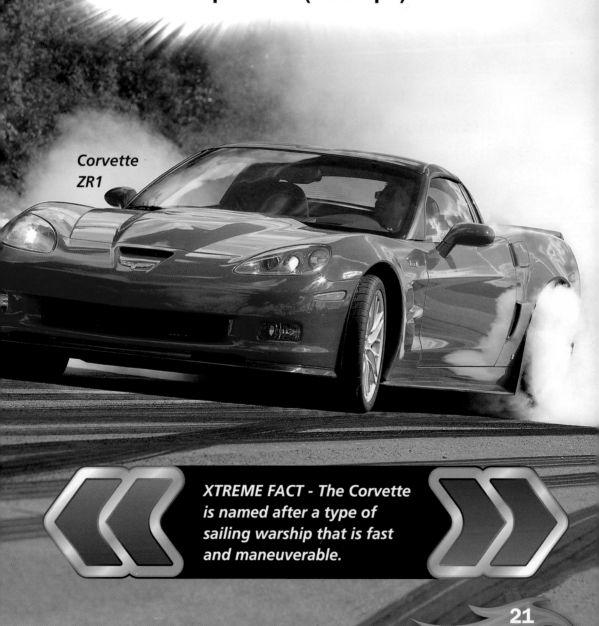

Corvette ZR1

XTREME FACT - The Corvette is named after a type of sailing warship that is fast and maneuverable.

FAMOUS SPORTS CARS

Ford GT — The Ford GT40 was a legendary car that won several races at the 24 Hours of Le Mans in France in the 1960s. In 2004, Ford released the GT, an updated design of the mid-engine sports car.

2005
Ford GT

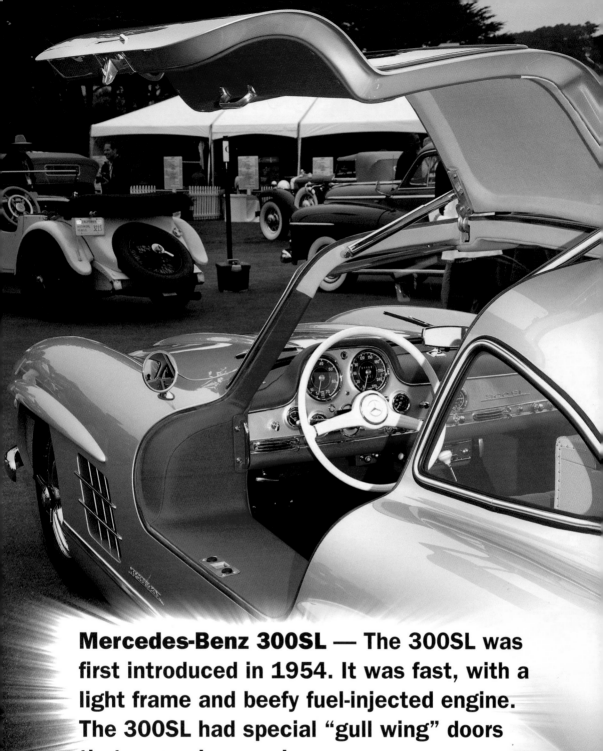

Mercedes-Benz 300SL — The 300SL was first introduced in 1954. It was fast, with a light frame and beefy fuel-injected engine. The 300SL had special "gull wing" doors that opened upwards.

McLaren MP4-12C — British car maker McLaren's 2012 MP4-12C is a supercar with a lightweight carbon-fiber body. Its 592-horsepower engine propels the car from 0 to 60 miles per hour (97 kph) in just 3.2 seconds.

McLaren MP4-12C

Nissan Skyline GT-R — Nicknamed "Godzilla," the Japanese Nissan Skyline GT-R dominated race tracks and the open road in the 1990s. The Skyline was featured in several movies, including *The Fast and the Furious* series. Its supercar successor today is simply called the GT-R.

Nissan GT-R with round "afterburner" taillights.

Bugatti Veyron — The French-made Bugatti Veyron has a 16-cylinder engine with four turbochargers. With a top speed of 268 miles per hour (431 kph), it is one of the fastest street-legal cars available. It is also the most expensive. The Super Sport model costs $2.4 million.

Bugatti Veyron

Lamborghini Aventador — The flagship of Italian automaker Lamborghini, the Aventador impresses sports car lovers with its stunning looks and high performance.

Lamborghini Aventador

Mazda Miata MX-5 — This quick and affordable Japanese roadster is the best-selling sports car ever, with more than 900,000 sold worldwide through 2011.

Mazda Miata MX-5

SRT Viper

Enzo Ferrari

AC Shelby Cobra

**BMW
Mini Cooper**

5873 GRV

Audi R8

Lamborghini Diablo

29

GLOSSARY

Aerodynamic
Something that has a shape that reduces the drag, or resistance, of air moving across its surface. Racing cars that have aerodynamic shapes can go faster because they don't have to push as hard to get through the air.

Driveshaft
A large rotating shaft that transmits power from the transmission to the wheels.

Horsepower
Horsepower is a unit of measure of power. The term was originally invented to compare the power output by a steam engine with that of an average draft horse.

Roadster
A roadster is usually defined as a small, sporty car that handles well, and has a soft-top that can be opened (a convertible). Some modern roadsters have hard tops that are retractable.

Supercharge
A supercharger compresses air and forces it into the combustion chambers, or engine cylinders. (The process is called forced air induction.) With this added oxygen,

more fuel can be added, which creates a bigger explosion in the chamber and gives the engine more power than it would have normally.

Transmission
A set of gears and shafts that transmits power from the engine to the axles, where the wheels are located.

Turbocharge
Turbochargers use the power of exhaust gasses to power a compressor that injects additional air into the engine cylinders. Turbochargers are usually more efficient than superchargers.

Wheelbase
The distance between the front and rear axles on a vehicle. Many sports cars have short wheelbases, which give the vehicles better handling and control.

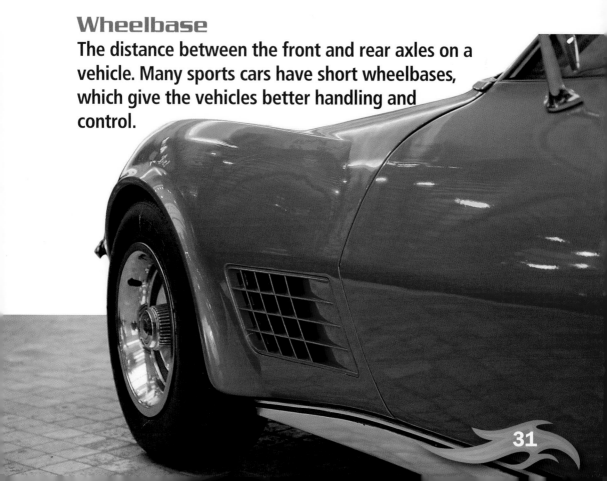

INDEX